Christopher Barker

Certain Prayers Set forth by Authority to be Used for the Prosperous Success

Of he Majesties Forces and Navy

Christopher Barker

Certain Prayers Set forth by Authority to be Used for the Prosperous Success
Of he Majesties Forces and Navy

ISBN/EAN: 9783744707695

Printed in Europe, USA, Canada, Australia, Japan

Cover: Foto ©Lupo / pixelio.de

More available books at **www.hansebooks.com**

Certaine Prayers
set foorth by Autho-
ritie, to be vsed for the
prosperous successe
of her Maiesties
Forces and
Nauy.

Imprinted at London,
by the Deputies of Chri-
stopher Barker, Prin-
ter to the Queenes
most excellent
Maiestie.

1597.

HVMILITAS

DIEV ET MON DROIT

GOD all-maker, keeper, and guider: Inurement of thy rare-seene, vnused, & seeld-heard-of goodnesse; powred in so plentiful sort vpon vs full oft, breeds now this boldnes, to craue with bowed knees, and hearts of humilitie, thy large hand of helping power, to afsist with wonder our iust cause, not founded on Prides-motion, nor begun on Malice-stock; But as thou best knowest, to whom nought is hid, grounded on iust defence from wrongs, hate, and bloody desire of conquest. For since, meanes thou hast imparted to saue that thou hast giuen, by enioying

A.iii.   such

such a people, as scornes their blood-shed, where suretie ours is one: Fortifie (deare G o D) such hearts in such sort, as their best part may be worst, that to the truest part meant worst, with least losse to such a Nation, as despise their liues for their Countreys good. That all Forreine lands may laud & admire the Omnipotencie of thy worke: a fact alone for thee only to performe. So shall thy Name be spread for wonders wrought, and the faithfull encouraged, to repose in thy vnfellowed Grace: And we that minded nought but right, inchained in thy bonds for perpetuall slauerie, and liue & die the sacrificers of our soules for such obteined fauour. Warrant, deare Lord, all this with thy command.

A m e n.

Ost mighty God and mercifull Father, as hitherto of thyne infinite goodnes thou hast very miraculously protected thy humble Seruant our Soueraigne Lady & Queene, and all vs her subiects the people of her Dominions, frō many dangerous conspiracies, malicious attempts, and wicked designements of her and our very obstinate & implacable enemies : Forasmuch as they stil continewing their malice, & preparing their Forces to assaile vs both by Land & Sea, thou (O Lord) to withstand their furie, hast stirred vp the heart of thine Anoynted our Soueraigne, to send out some of her Forces for our defence : we thine vnworthy seruants doe most humbly beseech thee, through the merites of our Sauiour Christ, so to conduct them, encourage them,

B

them, and defend them with thy strong
and mightie arme, as that whatsoeuer
they shall attempt and take in hand for
defence of this Realme against her ene=
mies, may prosper and haue most happy
successe. Direct & leade them (O Lord)
in safetie, strengthen their Gouernours
and Leaders with sound counsell and
valiant resolution. Blesse their conflicts
with notable victories both by Sea and
Land: preserue them from all contagi-
on and mortalitie either by Sworde or
sicknesse, and giue vnto them (O Lord)
if it be thy blessed will, such an honoura=
ble and happy returne, as may tend to
our defence by cōfusion of our enemies,
to the renowme & comfort of our Soueraigne, to the benefite of thy Church,
to the good of this Kingdome, and to
the prayse and glory of thy most mighty
Name, through Iesu Christ our Lord:
To whom with thee and the holy
Ghost be ascribed all honour,
power, and dominion,
both nowe and for
euer. Amen.

O most

Most mightie GOD, and Lorde of Hostes, which reignest ouer all the Kingdomes of the world, who hast power in thine hand to saue thy chosen, & to iudge thine Enemies, and in all ages hast giuen great and glorious Victories vnto thy Church, with small handfuls ouerthrowing great multitudes and terrible Armies: Let thine eares be now attent vnto our prayers, and thy mercifull eye vpon this Realme & kingdome. And as of thine vnspeakeable goodnes thou hast blessed vs with infinite and extraordinary blessings, all the yeres of her Maiesties most happy reigne ouer vs, and of late hast also myraculously deliuered vs from sundry the bloody practises of our very implacable enemies: So now, we humbly beseech thee (O mercifull Father) to ayde vs with thy mighty Arme in this our present iust cause, waging warre not in pride or ambition of mind, or any other worldly respect, but onely for the necessary defence

B.ii.   of

of Religion, our liues, and Countrey. Be mercifull therefore, O Lord, to our present Forces, and passing ouer both their transgressions and ours, prosper them both by Sea and land. Giue our Leaders & companies, the strength of Unicornes, the hearts of Lyons, armies of steele, hands of iron, and feete of flint, to beate and tread downe all thine enemies and ours. Let thine helpe from aboue at this time strengthen our Nauy and Armie, thy mercie ouershadowe them, thy power as a wall of fire enuyron them, thy wisedome direct them, thy prouidence secure them, thine holy Angels garde them, thy Sonne our Lorde Jesus Christ stand vp for them, and thy Justice confound, and Maiestie ouerwhelme all aduersarie power exalting it selfe against this land and thy Gospel. That all the world may know, that it is thy fauour that prospereth, thy blessing that preserueth, and thine arme that ouercommeth in the day of battell. So we that be thy people and sheepe of thy folde, shall sing vnto thy glorie the songs of prayse and thankesgiuing, and magnifie

magnifie thy goodneſſe in the midſt of thine holy Temple for euer, through Ieſus Chriſt our Lord, our onely Saniour and Mediatour. Amen.

O Almightie Lorde God of Hoſtes, it is thine owne gracious promiſe, that when thy people ſhall go out to battell againſt their enemies, by the way þ thou ſhalt ſend them, & ſhall call vpon thee for thy holy helpe, that then thou (Lord) wilt heare their prayers in heauen, and iudge their cauſe: In aſſured truſt of this thy good promiſe, we preſent this our ſupplication before thee. O Lorde iudge thou our cauſe, iudge thou betweene vs and our cruell enemies. Thou ſeeſt Lorde, that they firſt inuaded vs, and ſo doe ſtill continue, and not wee them: that they firſt conſpired to root vs out, that we might be no more a people of English birth, and

B.iii.   that

that then though thou from heauen diddest shew thy selfe, in scattering their proud forces, to be displeased with their attempt, yet notwithstanding by mightie preparations at this present they seeke our ruine still. That which armeth vs, is neither desire of enlarging our owne borders, nor thirst of blood, nor rauine of spoyle, but onely our owne iust defence, onely to breake the power of our enemies, and to turne away the battell from our owne gates : For that if we sit still, and suffer them to gather strength, they will suddenly make a breach vpon vs, and destroy the mother with the children. This they seeke, O Lord, & as thou seest, that the heart of thine Anointed in all her actions is vpright before thee, so mainteine thou our right, & be enemie to our enemies. Great is their malice (as thou Lord seest) and great is y̆ mischiefe they intend against vs. Let not the wicked haue their desire : O Lord, let not their mischieuous imaginations prosper, least they be too proude. And albeit our many and grieuous iniquities may testifie against vs,

and

and iustly deserue that thou shouldest make the enemies sword the auenger of thy couenant which wee haue broken: Yet deale thou with vs according to thy mercy, O Lord. We haue sinned, Lord, doe thou vnto vs what seemeth good in thine eyes: onely at this time wee pray thee to succour vs, and not make vs a scorne and derision to our oppressers. The rather O Lord, for that wee put not our trust in any strength of our owne, but our eyes looke onely to thee. We know, Lord, the battell is thine, and that with thee it is nothing to saue with many, or with few: For that except thou command the winds, we can not stirre, and except thou blesse with counsell and courage, wee shall not preuaile, and all these are in thine handes to giue or to withholde. Helpe vs, O Lord God, for we rest on thee, and in thy Name go we foorth against these mightie preparations. O Lorde thou art our God, let not man preuaile against thee: let thine arme rise vp, and put on strength to preserue vs nowe as of olde, euen the same arme that was mightie for vs and a-

gainst

gainſt them in their former pride and furie.

Wherefore from thy holy Sanctuarie, O Lorde, open thine eyes and behold, incline thine eare and heare the prayer of thy ſeruants. Goe foorth, O Lord, with our Hoſtes by Sea and by land. Send forth the windes out of thy treaſures to bring them to the place appointed. Take all contagious ſickneſſe from the middeſt of them, O Lord the ſtrength of our ſaluation. Couer their heads in the day of battell. Send thy feare before thy ſeruants, & make their enemies to flee and fal before them. Let thy faith (Lord) make them valiant in battell, and put to flight the Armies of Aliens. And by this ſhall we know, O Lorde, that thou fauoureſt vs, in that our enemie doeth not triumph ouer vs, and ſhall alwayes confeſſe to the prayſe of thy Name, that it was thy hand, and that it was thou, Lord, the ſhield of our helpe, and ſword of our glory, that haſt done theſe great things for vs, and euermore ſay, Prayſed be the Lorde, that hath pleaſure in the proſperitie of his seruants. Heare vs, O Lord for the glorie of thy Name, for thy louing Mercie, and for thy trueth sake, euen for the merites and intercession of our Lord Jesus Christ. Amen.

Eternall God in power most mighty, in strength most glorious, without whom the Horse & Chariot is in vaine prepared against ye day of battell: vouchsafe (wee beseeche thee) from thy high throne of Maiestie, to heare and receiue the heartie & humble prayers, which on bended knees, we ye people of thy pasture and sheepe of thy hands, doe in an vnfayned acknowledgement of thy might and our owne weakenesse, powre out before thee on the behalfe of our gratious Soueraigne, and on the behalfe of her Armies, her Nobles, her Valiants, and men of warre: who by thee inspired haue put their liues in their hands, and at this time doe oppose themselues, against the malice and violence of such, as beare a mortall hate at thy Sion, and doe dayly conspire and rise vp against it,

euen againſt the Church, thine Annoin-
ted, and the people of this her Land. A-
riſe then (O Lord) and ſtand vp we pray
thee, to helpe and defend them : be thou
their Captaine to goe in and out before
them, and to leade them in this iourney:
teache their fingers to fight, and their
hands to make battaile. The Generall
and Chieftaines bleſſe with the ſpirite
of wiſedome, counſell, and direction: the
Souldiers with mindes ready to performe and execute. Gird them all with
ſtrength, and powre out vpon them the
ſpirite of courage : giue them in the day
of battell, heartes like the hearts of Li-
ons, inuincible and feareleſſe againſt
euill, but terrible to ſuch as come out a-
gainſt them. Where the enemie doeth
rage, and danger approche, be thou (O
Lord) a rocke of ſaluation, and a tower
of defence vnto them. Breake the enemies weapons : As ſmoke vaniſheth, ſo
let their enemies be ſcattered, and ſuch
as hate them, flie before them. Thou
ſeeſt (O Lord) the malice of our aduer-
ſaries, howe for thy Name which is called on ouer vs, and for the trueth of thy

would liue in peace. Stirre vp therefore (O Lord) thy strength, and auenge
our iust quarrell: turne the sword of our
enemie vpon his owne head, and cause
his delight in warre to become his
owne destruction : As thou hast dealt
with him heretofore, so now scatter his
Forces, and spoile his mighty Ships, in
which he trusteth. So shall we the people of thine inheritance, giue praise vnto
thy Name, and for thy great mercy giue
thankes vnto thee in the great Congregation: yea, the World shall know, and
the Nations shall vnderstand to the
praise of thy glory, that thou alone defendest them that trust in thee, and giuest victorie vnto Princes. Heare vs (O
Lord our strength) in these our prayers
for Iesus Christ his sake. Amen.

Almighty God, which onely
doest great wonders, shewe
foorth (we pray thee) at this
time the power of thy might,

and

on the Sea, and by helping them in the day of battell, against the rage and violence of the Aduersarie. Thou seest (O Lord) that not for any worldly respects, but for the defence of this Realme, and the peace of thy Church in it, this iourney is vndertaken, to abate & withstand the pride, and to daunt the insolencies of our enemies, who conspire and bandie themselues against vs, breathing out wrath and vtter subuersion. Arise therefore wee pray thee (O Lord of Hostes) vnto our helpe, & let our enemies feele that thou still defendest our iust cause, and in ye day of battell doest fight for vs. Not in our owne sword, nor in the arme of our owne flesh, doe we put our trust, but our trust is in the multitude of thy mercies, & in the strength of thy mightie Arme, who art God alone. Blesse therefore the Chieftaines & Leaders of our bands, with ye spirit of wisedome, counsell, and magnanimitie, and the Souldiers with courage and fortitude, to stand bndaunted, & without feare in the day of battell. But as for their enemies, and such as come out against them, cast a feare & astonishment vpon them, that they may fal, and couer their faces with shame & confusion. That all the worlde may know, that thou (O God) resistest the proude and wicked men, and that thou auengest the cause of such, as put their trust in thee. Heare vs, O God of Hostes, euen for Christ his sake our only Sauiour and Redeemer. Amen.

O God most glorious, ye shield of al that trust in thee, who alone doest sende Peace to thy people, and causest warre to cease in all the world, Consider the dayly troubles of thy seruants, & behold the malice of our Aduersaries, who for thy Names sake, which is called on ouer vs, and for the trueth of thy Gospel wherin we reioyce, doe conspire & band them selues against vs, breathing out wrath and vtter sub=uersion. Many a time hath their wrath bene kindled, so that they would haue

swallowed

swallowed vs vp quicke : but by thy power their purpose hath bene frustra= ted, their counsels preuented , their pre= parations ouerthrowen, and we deliue= red. Yet, O Lorde, their heart is set a= gainst vs , still to vexe & trouble vs that faine would liue in peace. But for the quiet of thy Church, and that thine ene= mies may knowe thee to be a God of mercy, cause them to returne at last, and not any longer to hate those whome thou hast loued : Make them to see that their plotts & designements are against thee , who for vs fightest against them, drowning their ships , & casting downe their strong holdes in which they doe trust : that thy Name may be glorified in the day of their conuersion. But if they shall still harden their hearts , and will not vnderstand either our defence, or their owne calamitie to come of thee: Make voyde their deuises, disclose their counsels, discouer their secret complots, that in the snare which they haue layd for vs , their owne feete may be taken. Finally, O Lord, whensoeuer they pre= pare them selues to battaile , take the defence

set forth by Authoritie.

defence of our iuſt cauſe into thine hand: Breake their Nauies, diſperſe their Armies, and caſt vpon them a feare and aſtoniſhment, that they may tremble at thy preſence, and flye before they be pur= ſued: Graunt this O Lord our ſtrength euen for Chriſt his ſake. Amen.

Eternall God, Lord of the whole worlde, and guide of Sea and Land, who by thy mightie power ſorteſt to what effect thou wilt, the Councels and actions of all men: gratiouſly vouch= ſafe to bleſſe & order vnto happy iſſue, the late begunne worke of our gratious Soueraigne, in the hand of her Nobles and men of warre, nowe ſent out by Seas, to withſtande the Enemies of her life, her people, and thy Church. As Guide and Generall of the iourney, let it pleaſe thee (mightie Lorde of Hoſtes) to goe in and out before them, giue light to direct their steps, and in a pillar of a Cloude defend them. Put vpon them thy spirit of Counsell and fortitude, & vnder the banner of thy power and protection, let the worke be effected. Courage and imbolden them in the day of conflict, to stand vndaunted & without feare. Make way and opportunitie for them to attempt with aduantage, and for thy Names sake graunt(O glorious God) to their puissant attempts happy successe in battell, to their battell a ioyfull victorie, and to their victorie a safe and triumphant returne. So will we y̶ people of thine inheritance, which nowe pray for the blessing of thy grace vpon them, praise thy Name for euer, & together with them ascribe both cause and glory of the worke, not to our owne strength, but vnto thy power, who alone giuest victory in the day of battell: and for thy great mercies will giue thankes vnto thee in the midst of the Congregation. Heare vs, O Father, euē for Christ his sake. Amen.

FINIS.